In By The Half

A play

Jimmie Chinn

Samuel French—London
New York-Toronto-Hollywood

ISBN 0 573 12126 5

Please see page iv for further copyright information

CHARACTERS

Madam, an elderly actress
Doris, her housekeeper, slightly younger than Madam
Doctor, male or female, any age
Sylvia, young
Ursula, early forties

The action takes place in the sitting room of Madam's
small, neat, terraced cottage in Hammersmith, West
London

Time — the present

IN BY THE HALF

First performed by Teddington Theatre Club Audio
with the following cast:

Madam	Jennifer Laney
Doris	Doris Winsborrow
Doctor*	Jack Smerdon
Sylvia	Catherine Early
Ursula	Merlyn Lowther

Directed by Ken Mason
Incidental Music by Ken Mason, sung by Wendy
Bedford

* Please note that, though the Doctor was originally
played by a male actor and is male in the text, it is
possible, and perfectly acceptable, for this character
to be played by a woman.

For Rachel Kempson

IN BY THE HALF

The sitting room of Madam's small, neat terraced cottage in Hammersmith, West London

An archway L *leads out to a small hall, the stairs and the front door (which are unseen). A door* R *leads to a small kitchen. Through a window a small untidy garden can be seen and there is a fireplace in the 'fourth wall'*

The living-room furniture and furnishings are old-fashioned but well-kept and suggest a more elegant time and place. There are two armchairs, a chaise-longue and a small polished dining table

The CURTAIN *rises on darkness. Music plays. The Lights slowly come up to reveal the table laid for breakfast, including a plate of scrambled eggs. The door to the kitchen is open. Madam is seated at the table, wearing her dressing-gown and glasses and reading a copy of* The Times. *Although she is very elderly, she still has the look and authority of a once quite distinguished actress*

The music fades; as it does so, we hear a grandfather clock (unseen) begin to strike the half hour

Doris enters from the kitchen. Younger than her employer, she was once Madam's dresser and is now her housekeeper and companion. She wears a wrap-around overall and is carrying a tray, a Hoover and four letters. She starts to clear the table, working thoughout the following exchange

Madam (*peering at Doris over her glasses*) This is outrageous! It says here that I'm dead!

Doris (*with no interest*) You haven't finished your breakfast.

Madam (*reading*) 'Quietly, at her home in Sussex. She was eighty-four.' (*To Doris*) Absolute rubbish!

Doris Honestly, I go to the trouble of making scrambled eggs and what happens? You've hardly touched it.

Madam Well, I'm not taking this lying down. I shall write a stiff letter. This afternoon, after lunch. How can they think I'm dead?

Doris Good money down the drain, is this. You'll get no egg at all tomorrow and see how you like that. More tea?

Madam They're obviously mixing me up with Dorothy Bickerstaff. Now she *did* live in Sussex.

Doris (*picking up the teapot*) More tea or not? This is the last call.

Madam I shall ring the editor. I know him. His mother was Lady Flockley — Harriet Skinner before she married. The worst Juliet I've ever had the misfortune to sit through. I shan't have any more tea; it was far too weak.

Doris (*putting more things on the tray*) Too weak, too strong, too hot, too cold; I get giddy with it all.

Madam We don't live in Sussex, do we?

Doris I wish you'd pull yourself together. We live in Hammersmith.

Madam Is that in Sussex?

Doris I shall be doing your bedroom this morning so I hope you haven't left it in a tip.

Madam I shall require writing paper and envelopes. The white, I think. I save the blue for letters of a more intimate nature.

Doris The doctor's due at ten, don't forget, so you'll need clean knicks and things.

Madam Doris, I do wish you wouldn't constantly refer to my undergarments: it's sordid. Have you read this obituary?

Doris I read the *Daily Mirror*, you know that. You don't get obituaries in there. (*She plugs in the Hoover*)

Madam I suppose no-one ever dies in the *Daily Mirror*.

Doris switches the Hoover on and moves quickly round the room with it

(*Raising her voice*) Must you do that now?

Doris And remember I have to go out this morning, so I'll leave your lunch — cold — between two plates in the fridge, and I don't want you touching it before one o'clock, right?

Madam Out? You're always out. Where to?

Doris Now don't start. You know perfectly well 'where to'; I always visit my sister Dolly on Saturdays. There's another beside you who calls for my attention.

Madam How on earth am I expected to remember what my maid does on a Saturday?

Doris Oh, I see. 'Maid' today, is it? What's happened to 'housekeeper' all of a sudden?

Madam (*as if suddenly deaf*) I'm sorry ... ?

Doris If I recall, all those years ago I was employed as your dresser-companion. 'No household duties', the advert said. I never flaming well stop!

Madam Well, it's most inconvenient. When will you be back?

Doris (*switching off the Hoover and winding up the flex*) Before curtain-up, so keep your hair on.

Madam I must be ready by the half so that I can have my lie down.

Doris You'll be the death of me, you will.

Madam What did you say?

Doris (*handing Madam the four letters*) Here's your post. Two bills, one circular and one from your Ursula.

Madam (*putting the letters on the table and ignoring them*) How do you know that? You've been steaming open my letters again.

Doris I don't need to steam open anything. I know the handwriting. She'll be after money again, mark my words.

Madam It's none of your business.

Doris It soon will be. When you've no money left to pay my wages and I have to leave you high and dry. I don't work for nothing, you know. I'm not a sodding charity!

Madam I can't hear a word you say. You must learn to enunciate properly. Project. All these years in the theatre and you've learned nothing.

Doris (*projecting her voice and enunciating clearly*) I said I am not a sodding charity!

Madam You see. What a glorious line. You must use it. Take a deep breath, fill the diaphragm and 'Speak the speech as I pronounced it to you, trippingly on the tongue.' Now try again: 'I am not a sodding charity!'

Doris I should save all that for Sylvia; she'll be here at twelve.

Madam Sylvia. Who is Sylvia?

Doris You know perfectly well who Sylvia is so stop being grand. She's your pupil — Saturday mornings, twelve till one.

Madam She's useless. Couldn't act her way out of a paper bag.

Doris Yes, well, don't tell her that. You need the money. *We* need the money.

Madam Where's my tea? You've cleared away my tea, woman.

Doris And please don't call me 'woman' — you know it gets my back up.

Madam I suppose it was you who told this wretched newspaper I was dead. For spite.

Doris Now, come along. Bathroom please. A nice bath and change into those lovely clean undies in case the doctor wants to look at you.

Madam I refuse to be 'looked at.'

Doris You're an actress. You should be used to being looked at.

Madam Not in my underclothes.

Doris I don't see why not. They all strip off these days. You see it all the time on the telly. (*She relishes the next line, aware of the feelings it will produce*) Even your daughter.

Madam (*reacting to this sore point*) Please don't mention that to me. I was disgusted. Ashamed. 'A very important part', she said. And what did it turn out to be? A corpse — stark naked on a bed!

Doris Well, it was important — the whole play was about her, wasn't it — and no lines to learn. I thought she was ever so good.

Madam Of course she wasn't good. Ursula, sadly, has never been good in anything.

Doris You wait; next time I see her I shall tell her what you said.

Madam She knows what I think. When it came to handing out talent, Dame Fortune passed my daughter by. Have I had my breakfast? I'm peckish.

Doris (*folding the tablecloth*) Too late. No more food till lunchtime.

Madam I shall tell the doctor you starve me. Deprive me of food. Hide away my sweeties. You'll be reported to the authorities.

Doris (*collecting the tray*) Yes, yes, we've heard it all before.

Doris exits to the kitchen with the tray

Madam (*calling to Doris*) What am I playing tonight?

Doris (*off*) Mother Courage — on ice!

Madam I hate it. Dragging that great cart around the stage exhausts me. I must ask the stage manager to oil the wheels.

The front doorbell rings

Who's that at this time? I'm not even dressed.

Doris enters from the kitchen wiping her hands on a tea towel

Doris Keep your hair on. They've probably sent round a strait-jacket for you.

Doris exits into the hall

Madam (*calling out again*) I'm signing no autographs. Tell them I'm resting. Tell them that, according to this, I'm dead!
Doris (*off*) Oh, Doctor, you're early; come in.
Doctor (*off*) I do hope it's convenient, Doris. I'd forgotten it's my day at the hospital.
Madam (*calling again*) If it's Sir Godfrey I'll see him. I want a word about his performance the other night. He's got to find more pace.

The Doctor enters carrying a doctor's bag

Madam Oh, it's you!
Doctor Good-morning, Eleanor; hope I haven't caught you on the hop.
Madam I don't want you. I'm not ill. I'm an actress; actresses of my calibre are never ill.
Doctor I must say you're looking terribly well, dear. (*He winks at Doris*) Doris looking after you, is she? (*He opens the bag and brings out a stethoscope, pad and pen*)
Madam If it was left to her I'd have been dead years ago. I refuse to be injected.
Doctor No injections today. Just my little stethoscope. How's your chest?
Madam My chest is none of your business.

Doctor (*moving a chair to Madam's side and sitting*) No problem. There we are — nice deep breath.

Doris Oh, by the way, Doctor, she's in the obituaries again this morning. It's getting beyond a joke.

Doctor (*turning his head away from the patient and lowering his voice*) I shouldn't let it worry you, Doris. She's not half as silly as she makes out.

Doris exits to the kitchen. We hear the sounds of washing up during the following

Madam Why are you two whispering? Is it a cancer?

Doctor Afraid not, dear — a bit of congestion, that's all. Another deep breath.

Madam breathes deeply

(*Making small talk*) Terrible notice in *The Times* for the new *Merchant* at Stratford. He slaughters poor Shylock.

Madam Good. Who's playing it?

Doctor Some new chap, apparently. A performance you could put between two slices of bread by all accounts. One more deep one, dear.

Madam Off the television, I expect. No training — no experience — no talent! (*She breathes in deeply once more*)

Doctor Splendid. There really is a great improvement. How are the tablets?

Madam As usual. No good whatsoever. (*She lowers her voice*) Doris has got to go, Doctor. She's getting past it. My meals are late, undercooked — and she's so forgetful. Last night she was even late with my costume change in Act Three.

Doctor (*re-packing his bag*) Oh, dear ...

Madam I know what it is — she wanted to ruin my performance. She knew the critics were in.

Doctor (*not taking any of this seriously*) You could always sack
   her I suppose.

Madam But where would she go? You know she's been with me
   for years. How could I be so heartless?

Doctor Yes, well, that is how it might appear, Eleanor.

Madam Of course, she is far too old; that's the top and bottom
   of it.

Doctor (*trying not to sound sarcastic*) Ten years younger than
   you if I'm not mistaken.

Madam She's got her bus pass, I know that for a fact. She goes
   all the way to see her sister Dolly for nothing. And the cinema
   — half price for the matinee. And, I hate to mention it, but
   she's developed a sordid fixation about my underclothes.

Doctor I shouldn't let it worry you, dear. The moment she starts
   trying to climb into bed with you we'll have a little word with
   her. Heard from Ursula?

Madam When, I ask you, do I ever hear from her?

Doctor Saw her on television the other night. Jolly good, I
   thought. A bit too thin, perhaps.

Madam How she can bear the family name and appear in
   rubbish like that is beyond me. We've always stuck to the
   classics.

Doctor It may be all she's offered, Eleanor.

Madam Are you surprised? I have never appeared on television—and I never shall.

Doris enters with clean bed linen

Doris Can I get you anything, Doctor?

Madam Tea and biscuits, please — at once!

Doris Not for you. I was asking the doctor.

Doctor No, thank you, Doris. Must dash.

Madam I've been telling the doctor how incompetent you're
   becoming.

Doris Oh, yes.

Madam We both agree you're past it. You should be put out to graze, thrown on the scrap heap. Isn't that what you said, Doctor?

Doctor (*writing on her pad*) I'm writing a prescription for more tablets, Doris. She must be running short.

Doris Thanks. I'll get them on my way to Dolly's.

Madam I never see any tablets. She hoards them. Waiting till she has hundreds — then she can poison me with them.

Doris Time for your bath, otherwise you'll have Sylvia here — and she won't want to see your sagging bosoms.

Madam (*rising from the table*) See what I mean, Doctor? This isn't a normal person speaking.

Doctor I'll pop in next week, Eleanor. Don't overdo things. And *no* sweeties *or* chocolate!

Madam Don't do this, don't do that — my life is a misery. I shall go over my lines for tonight and leave you to talk about me. I know what goes on behind my back. (*She heads towards the hall door, quoting loudly as she goes*)

> 'O pardon me, thou bleeding piece of earth,
>
> That I am meek and gentle with these butchers.'

Doctor (*laughing*) You're a saint, Doris. I've no idea how you stick it.

Doris She don't get any better an' that's a fact. But she's harmless enough. I just hope to Gawd I don't end up like that. Who'd look after me?

Doctor You've always got your sister I suppose.

Doris You must be mad! Dolly's nearly as bad as her. Is Madam really better?

Doctor Strong as a horse, dear. It's all play-acting. It's how she passes her time.

Doris Every night, about seven o'clock, she still thinks she's about to go on stage, you know. I have to get her ready, call the 'half', then 'beginners, please'. Sad, really.

Doctor If only Ursula could visit more often.

Doris (*scornfully*) She won't come. Not unless it's to borrow more money. There's a letter from her on the table. Unopened of course. Madam never reads 'em.

Doctor Ah, well — none of our business, I suppose. Must be off, dear. See you next week.

Music begins to play

Doris I'll show you out.

They exit to the hall, Doris still carrying the clean bedclothes

The Lights fade to Black-out

The music swells; the sound of the grandfather clock striking another half mixes with the music, which then fades

The Lights come up again

Rain is falling outside

It is three hours later. Madam, dressed for the day, is standing by the chaise longue reciting a voice exercise. Sylvia, a plain, awkward and spotty girl with voice problems, including an inability to pronounce her 'R's, a cold and thick glasses, is seated on the chaise longue. She has a coat, hat and bag with her

Madam (*declaiming rather dramatically*) 'What a to-do to die today at a minute or two to two — A thing distinctly hard to say but a harder thing to do!'

Sylvia (*trying her best but sounding pretty awful*) 'What a to-do to die today at a minute or two to two ——'

Madam (*offended by the awful sounds*) No, no, no, no, no,
Sylvia. Your voice sounds like something out of a tin — a
small horrid tin. Can't you do anything with it?

Sylvia I am trying, Madam.

Madam Listen to me. 'What a to-do ... to die today ... at a minute
or two to two.' Can you not hear the difference? The quality
of sound?

Sylvia I think so, Madam.

Madam To be an actress of outstanding quality one must have
a voice like a musical instrument. One should be able to play
upon it as though it were a cathedral organ.

Sylvia I've never heard a cathedral organ, Madam.

Madam Sylvia, are you trying to be facetious?

Sylvia I don't think so, Madam.

Madam (*moving about the room dramatically*) Try this: 'Around
the rugged rocks the ragged rascal ran.'

Sylvia (*rising and making gestures like her teacher*) 'Around
the rugged rocks the ragged rascal ran.'

Madam (*trying to be patient*) I see. We seem to have a problem
here. Sit down, dear. We'll try something else.

Sylvia sits

What about this? 'Betty Botter bought some butter for to make
her batter better but this butter only made her batter bitter!' Say
it, Sylvia.

Sylvia (*now terrified*) Better.

Madam (*closing her eyes*) Betty ...

Sylvia Betty Batter ...

Madam Botter ...

Sylvia Batty Bitter bought some batter ...

Madam Sylvia, the woman's name is Betty Botter and she
bought some butter for to make her batter better!

Sylvia (*crying*) It's no good, Madam — I'm useless.

Madam I thought you wanted to play Juliet one day.

Sylvia I do, Madam, I do. But I'm not any good.

Madam Well, don't cry. Don't get upset. It isn't that important, Sylvia.

Sylvia But it is, Madam. It's very important. To me. I want to be on the stage — like you, Madam.

Madam Well, fine. Fine, Sylvia. But perhaps we should set our sights a little lower than Juliet.

Sylvia But I know the lines an' everything, Madam.

Madam (*sitting beside Sylvia and putting her arm around her*) Listen to me, Sylvia. An actress, a truly great actress, must know her limitations, dear. I mean, look at me; I couldn't, for instance, play — well, I couldn't play ...

Sylvia (*blowing her nose*) You see — you can't think of anything. And that's because you're a wonderful actress. My teacher says so.

Madam (*impressed*) Does he really. What's his name?

Sylvia 'She', Madam. My English teacher's a 'she'. Miss Tentilow. She goes to the theatre all the time and she's seen you.

Madam Not for rather a long time, I'm afraid.

Sylvia But she has seen you, Madam. She saw you up West in 'The Apple Garden'.

Madam I think you mean *The Cherry Orchard*, Sylvia.

Sylvia That's it. She said you played in all sorts of plays, Madam.

Madam She must be rather elderly — your teacher.

Sylvia She is. She's dead ancient. But she's a smashing teacher. I told her you was giving me lessons to be an actress and she was very impressed.

Madam (*distantly*) I see.

Sylvia Shall we try again, Madam?

Madam I'm sorry ... ?

Sylvia Here, you all right, Madam?

Madam Yes, Sylvia, I'm fine, dear.

Sylvia I can do 'Horace', Madam — I can do that one. 'Oh, Horace, isn't it horrid, when you're hot and in a hurry, and you have to hold your hat on with your hand!' (*Proudly*) How's that?

Madam Well done. Very well done, Sylvia. I think you deserve a reward for that. What about some chocolate? Oh, dear, I do believe my housekeeper's forgotten to ...

Sylvia Don't worry, Madam, I brought you some. (*She produces a large bar of fruit and nut chocolate from her bag*) I know how much you like it.

Madam Sylvia, you're a very thoughtful student. By far the best one I have.

Sylvia I thought I was the only one you had.

Madam Are you? Perhaps you're right.

Sylvia It's fruit and nut, Madam, so I hope you haven't got dentures.

Madam (*taking the chocolate*) My teeth, thank God, are all mine. I did pay for most of them but they are mine. What an enormous bar of chocolate. Are we to share it? (*She tears the wrapping open*)

Sylvia Oh, no, it's all yours. I mustn't eat chocolate. It brings me out in spots.

Madam (*eating a piece of chocolate*) This is scrumptious, Sylvia. But you're very naughty — you mustn't go spending your pocket money on me.

Sylvia Why not? You won't take any money for my lessons and Mum says that's taking liberties and I wouldn't want to do that, would I?

Madam Your mum's really keen on you becoming an actress. She told me so. (*She eats more chocolate*)

Sylvia She'd like me to be like Madonna, Madam.

Madam Madonna? Madonna who?

Sylvia She's an actress, Madam. She's been in films an'

everything. (*She rises and moves to the window*) She sings an'
dances an' stuff like that ... (*She looks out into the garden*) Oh,
Madam ...

Madam What's the matter — what can you see?

Sylvia In your garden, Madam — there's a woman. She looks
ever so sad, just standing there in the rain.

Madam (*rising and moving to the window*) A woman. Are you
sure it's not Doris back from her sister's? (*She steps back from
the window*) Oh, my God!

Sylvia What's wrong?

Madam (*ashen*) It's her.

Sylvia Her?

Madam Ursula. My daughter. (*She panics*) If we hide, Sylvia,
we can pretend to be out. (*She crouches downstage of the
chaise longue*)

Sylvia Too late, madam. She's spotted me.

The doorbell rings

(*Crouching beside Madam*) Well?

Madam (*lowering her voice*) Well what?

Sylvia We can't just hide like this — you'll have to open the
door.

Madam I don't see why. It's my door — I can do with it as I
wish.

The doorbell rings again

Sylvia This isn't fair, Madam. I'm very embarrassed. She's seen
me. She might think I'm holding you prisoner, beating you up,
even. Teenagers round here have a terrible reputation, Madam.

Madam (*rising*) Oh, very well. Let her in. But I'm only doing
it for your sake. I shan't speak to her.

Sylvia gets up and exits to the hall

Madam adjusts her clothing in anticipation of the visit

Sylvia (*off*) Hallo, Miss. Madam's through here.
Ursula (*off*) Who are you?
Madam (*calling*) Tell her nothing, Sylvia. Tell her to mind her own business.
Ursula (*off*) Don't worry, I can handle Madam. I've been doing it most of my life.

Ursula enters. She is a thin and attractive, but tired- and careworn-looking woman in her early forties, smoking a cigarette and carrying a bag. Sylvia follows her on

(*Softly*) Hallo, Mother.
Madam (*turning away*) You're too late — I'm dead. It's in all the papers. I died quietly at my home in Sussex — aged eighty-four.

Sylvia looks puzzled by Madam's extraordinary performance

Ursula Where's Doris?
Madam I sacked her. She became far too eccentric. Staying out late, bringing strange men home, setting fire to things ... My doctor insisted on my giving her the elbow.
Sylvia (*embarrassed*) It's not true, Miss.
Ursula I'm sure it isn't. And who's this young lady?
Madam A neighbour's girl. She comes to borrow sugar.
Sylvia Oh, Madam, that's a fib. I'm her pupil, Miss. She teaches me to act.
Madam (*looking across at her daughter*) Yes, Sylvia. And, like my daughter here, you're not very good at it.

Ursula Save your insults, Mother.They hurt me no longer.

Sylvia (*impressed*) Here, hang on — didn't I see you on television? 'Inspector MacDougal Investigates', wasn't it? You were smashing, Miss.

Madam Smashing! She wasn't even alive. And most unsuitably attired.

Ursula I wrote to you, Mother. I said I was coming.

Madam I never received it. The post round here is so unreliable.

There is an awkward pause

I can offer you tea but nothing else.

Ursula Tea will be fine.

Madam Sylvia — tea please. For two. Now.

Sylvia Here, hang about, I can't make tea. My mum does all that in our house.

Madam Imagine you're my maid; it shouldn't be that difficult.

Sylvia I wouldn't know where to start, Madam.

Madam I thought you wanted to be an actress. Here's your chance — act! We'll have the Earl Grey, black, with a slice of lemon.

Sylvia Who's Earl Grey when he's at home?

Ursula Ordinary tea will do, Sylvia. My mother hates to admit that I've come down in the world.

Sylvia Oh, well, I can only try my best. But I can't guarantee nothing.

Sylvia exits to the kitchen

Madam (*calling to Sylvia*) The wooden tray, not the plastic, and a paper doily, please. We had to pawn the silver tray to buy food!

Ursula Save it, Mother. I'm sure your sense of **humour** is way above the girl's head.

Madam She's a simpleton. Her mother does our washing. But she's quite harmless. (*She pauses*) Why do you look at me like that?

Ursula I stood out there in the rain hoping, just this once, you might be pleased to see me.

Madam If it's money you're after — I haven't any.

Ursula I'm not in need of money this time.

Madam Don't tell me you're employed. Wonders will never cease.

Ursula I've just finished a tour. They didn't pay much but I managed to save.

Madam *Hamlet*? The Scottish play? *She Stoops ...* ? I've toured them all.

Ursula A terrible thriller, actually. I was gassed at the end of Act One.

Madam Fully clothed, I trust. You seem to be making a habit of dying early in the proceedings.

Ursula (*wearily; she is not up to her mother's sarcasm*) Mother, please, for the first time in our lives, could we talk about things that matter?

Madam The theatre has always mattered to me, Ursula. But then I was born to be an actress.

Ursula (*almost snapping*) Yes, and you've been doing it ever since, both on stage and off! (*She pauses, then speaks more quietly*) I'm sorry, I shouldn't have said that. No-one, but no-one, puts me in a temper like you do.

Madam (*sitting on the chaise longue*) Very well. If you insist. Let us speak of mundane matters. How's Roger?

Ursula His name was Robert, and he left me almost a year ago. It's Malcolm now.

Madam You seem to get through your men at a rate of knots. I was faithful to your father until the day he died. (*She glares at Ursula*) And he to me!

Ursula I refuse to rise to the bait, Mother. I'm not here to quarrel.

(*She pauses*) Am I allowed to say how well you're looking?

Madam I'm not. My doctor was only here this morning. Apparently I could go at any time. And why do you wear such unsuitable clothes? And your hair — it usedn't to be that colour. You should grow old gracefully; I'm not afraid to do so.

Ursula (*stubbing out her cigarette*) I'm tired. It's a long journey. May I sit?

Madam You look dreadful. And you're still smoking.

Ursula I can't help it. Anyway, it's too late now.

Madam Are you in trouble again?

Ursula (*putting her bag on the table and sitting*) No, I'm not in trouble.

Madam Unwell?

Ursula Mother, if you'd taken the time to read my letter ...

Sylvia enters from the kitchen, carrying a wooden tray with tea-cups and a milk jug clattering on it

Sylvia (*loudly*) The kettle's on and here's the cups. And no lemon — sorry. I've searched high and low.

Madam Quietly, Sylvia, quietly. If you want this job permanently you'll have to do better than this.

Sylvia I don't want the job at all, Madam. Where shall I put these?

Madam Put the tray on the table.

Sylvia does so; the cups clatter

Gently. And when you've brought the tea you may leave us. My daughter and I have things to discuss.

Sylvia You've changed your tune. She wasn't going to speak to you at all, Miss.

Madam That will do, Sylvia. I hope you've warmed the pot.

Sylvia Warmed the pot? What for?

Ursula (*rising*) Perhaps it would be simpler if I made the tea.

Ursula exits to the kitchen

Sylvia (*calling after Ursula*) I don't mind, Miss, honest. I was just beginning to get the hang of it.

Madam Sylvia, would you mind awfully if we cut our lesson short? I'll make it up to you next week.

Sylvia I don't mind. She seems ever so nice, Madam — your daughter. You can tell she belongs to you.

Madam She does try, Sylvia — but we haven't always seen eye to eye over the years.

Sylvia You shouldn't be too hard on her, Madam. She's all you've got and she doesn't look too well if you ask me.

Madam Sylvia, before you go, pass me that letter would you — on the table — and my glasses.

Sylvia (*fetching the letter*) This?

Madam (*taking the letter*) Thank you, dear.

Sylvia (*handing Madam the glasses*) Want me to open it for you?

Madam I can manage; I'm not completely senile. (*She puts on her glasses, tears open the envelope and reads the letter*)

Music creeps in, haunting and distant

Sylvia (*putting on her hat and coat*) I'll keep up with the exercises, Madam. I'll spend all week on 'Betty Botter'. I like that one; no R's in it, is there?

Madam is silent; she is too busy reading

Madam ... ? Oh, well, I'll see you next week ... I'll bring plain chocolate next time, I can see you don't like the nuts. Bye, Madam.

There is a pause

    Sylvia exits to the hall; we hear the front door slam behind her

Madam finishes the letter, removes her glasses and just stares into space for a moment. She is obviously very affected by what she has read and looks older, and weary

The grandfather clock strikes the hour; it is one o' clock

    Ursula enters quietly from the kitchen carrying the teapot. She stops and looks across at her mother

The music fades

Ursula (*quietly*) You've read it then.

There is a pause

    I'm sorry if it's come as a shock. Now you see why I thought it best to write it all down. Face to face, and being the bad actress I am, I'd have made it sound rather too melodramatic.

Madam (*still staring out*) I don't know what to say, Ursula.

Ursula Perhaps that you're sorry.

Madam Of course I am. But it seems so inadequate.

Ursula (*pouring tea*) These things happen every day. Foolishly we think they will never happen to us.

Madam How long have you known?

Ursula Several months.

Madam (*slightly angry*) And you never told me.

Ursula What was the point — what good would it have done?

Madam You've always been secretive. Even as a child. Even then you kept things from me.

Ursula (*handing Madam her tea*) Here, drink this, it'll do you good.

There is a silence. Ursula takes her tea and sits in an armchair

Madam (*at length*) When might this thing happen?

Ursula No-one can say for certain, but it can't be long now. I've had a couple of operations. I thought I was clear.

Madam (*angrily*) Operations? I'm your mother — I had a right to know.

Ursula The last thing I wanted was you at my bedside. Being dramatic; making a scene.

Madam (*looking at Ursula at last*) That isn't fair, Ursula.

Ursula I was instructed to rest, Mother. To avoid all forms of stress. We'd have been at each other's throats.

Madam Why must you always make me out to be a gorgon? I have feelings like everyone else.

Ursula Let's just say we agreed to keep it to ourselves and leave it at that.

Madam We?

Ursula The consultant and I. And my doctor, of course. I didn't want any fuss, Mother.

Madam But this Malcolm, what about him? Surely he should be told?

Ursula He won't be interested. Anyway, we don't live together. After Robert left I decided I was better on my own. Apart from which, Malcolm's an actor, he's working abroad — he wouldn't want his schedule disrupting.

Madam You speak of him so callously. Actors are the most caring people — he'd fly home at once.

Ursula Oh, come off it, Mother. Father? Caring?

Madam How dare you say that, Ursula. How dare you!

Ursula I'm sorry. I should learn to keep my mouth shut.

Madam Your father was always here when I needed him. It was you who disappeared — it was I who was left to pick up the pieces.

Ursula You admit there were pieces to be picked up, then? Why do you walk about with your eyes closed? Father didn't give that much for either of us and you know it!

Madam I refuse to speak of it. I was satisfied with my life. It was you who was always unable to hold a relationship together. Tom, Dick, Harry, Roger, Robert or whatever they called themselves — all of them fallen by the wayside. Have you never loved anyone?

Ursula (*quietly*) I've never been allowed to. I've always chosen people who cared only for themselves.

Madam I suppose I'm included in that. And your father?

Ursula (*rising and fetching her bag from the table*) I must have a cigarette.

Madam Cigarettes — and in your condition. Here, have some chocolate instead. (*She hands the partly-eaten chocolate bar to Ursula*)

Ursula I thought chocolate was banned in this house.

Madam It was a present. From Sylvia. She at least seems fond of me.

Ursula (*eating a piece of chocolate*) I hope you're not filling *her* head with all this theatrical nonsense.

Madam I'm helping to fulfill her dreams. Is there anything wrong in that?

Ursula What's the point if she isn't any good?

Madam She isn't. In fact, she's quite dreadful. It's a phase she's going through. One day she'll be content to work at Woolworth's. And, please, don't eat *all* the chocolate.

Ursula laughs

Why do you laugh?

Ursula You're still very funny. Cruel but funny.

Madam Cruel. How can you?

Ursula Perhaps that's what I should have done. Worked in a shop. I might have been happier.

Madam Nonsense. You could have been a good actress. Heaven knows we tried hard enough. Your father encouraged you, got you into drama school; I gave you the benefit of all my experience. You had great potential but you squandered it.

Ursula I was untalented, Mother. You should have seen that and pointed me elsewhere. I've spent my life in a profession for which I am unsuited.

Madam Rubbish. The theatre's in your blood. With dedication, commitment, you could have scaled the heights.

Ursula You're talking nonsense, Mother. I was always shy, inept, gawkish. It was obvious from the beginning, my first job, that I was never going to be any good. You should have been honest.

Madam You got the work. You wouldn't have been employed if they didn't think you had possibilities.

Ursula He was giving them money. They had to return the favour somehow.

Madam Please don't speak of your father like that.

Ursula It's true.

Madam I refuse to listen.

Ursula That seedy rep where I started — it was on its last legs. Father paid for that last season to go ahead; he even chose the plays.

Madam Splendid plays.

Ursula And as if that wasn't enough I even had to sleep with the director.

Madam (*furiously*) Ursula — your tongue!

Ursula I wouldn't be surprised if that was part of the deal.

Madam This is revolting. Charles Penwarren was a married man.

Ursula Charles Penwarren was a dirty old man. And I was
nineteen.

Madam I want you to go; leave this minute. I feel a 'turn'
coming on.

Ursula Why did you put me through all that?

Madam You're demented. Your illness is causing you to
ramble.

Ursula Father knew what was going on. I saw the way they
looked at each other. The nudges, the winks, the leers over a
double brandy in the theatre bar.

Madam I don't believe it. Your father? Charles Penwarren? I
knew his wife, a most respectable woman. She couldn't act but
she *was* respectable.

Ursula She at least was kind to me. She saw what was
happening.

Madam She fell down the stairs in *Heartbreak House* and never
worked again.

Ursula You don't listen, do you, Mother? You never did.
Anyway, none of it matters now and your tea's getting cold.

There is a silence, then the clock strikes a quarter past

Ursula (*looking out of the window*) The storm seems to be past;
it's stopped raining — there's even a shaft of sunshine. (*She
pauses*) Why do you choose to live here? It's so noisy — so
ugly.

Madam (*quietly*) It's all I can afford. The big house became a
liability. Too many bills — far too large to keep warm in
winter. Besides, Doris is getting on. This little house is perfect.
And it's close to town, the theatres, the art galleries.

Ursula (*gently amused*) You never go out.

Madam How do you know what I do with my life? You know
nothing.

Ursula Are you ever offered work?
Madam (*plainly lying*) All the time. The telephone never stops ringing. But the parts are all piffling.

There is a silence. Ursula looks out of the window

Madam (*at length, quietly*) Why did you come here?
Ursula (*without turning*) To tell you I was dying.
Madam You did that in the letter.
Ursula (*moved*) Perhaps I wanted to hear someone say I shall be missed.

There is a silence

(*With an effort*) Did you miss Father when he died?
Madam How can you ask such a dreadful question?
Ursula Please, Mother, I beg of you, be honest — just this once.
Madam Am I not always honest? (*She pauses, then continues, quietly, no longer on her dignity*) No. No, I didn't miss him. I didn't miss his drinking or his not coming home at nights. I didn't miss having to cover for him, having to sober him up to get him to the theatre by the half; his inability to remember his lines; his appalling behaviour in front of the entire company. I didn't miss his disgusting conduct with every young girl he came into contact with. And, most of all, I didn't miss his rudeness to me, his insults, his constant accusations, his jealousy when I got a good notice and he didn't. (*A beat*) No, I did not miss your father when he died, Ursula. (*A beat*) There, I've said it. I've finally said it.

There is a silence

Ursula (*simply, sincerely*) Thank you.

Madam I hope you're satisfied.

Ursula Is that why you shut me out? Because I saw all those things, because I saw and understood and felt sorry for you.

Madam I didn't need to be felt sorry for. (*A beat*) Is that why you never came to his funeral? I've never had the courage to ask you.

Ursula I wanted to come. For your sake. But it was easier to stay away.

Madam It doesn't matter. It was all so long ago. Life will go on. (*Her face registers that she has realized what she has said and she turns to look at Ursula*)

Ursula (*moving to sit beside Madam*) We've wasted so much time, you and I. All these years we could have been together; we could have been friends.

Madam I doubt it. I've grown far too selfish in my old age. I lead Doris a dance. Pretending to be ga-ga, demanding this and that. It's odd really: when your father died I was relieved not to have to play the role of the loving wife any longer, but here I am, acting a different part.

Ursula It's one of the penalties for an actress. You look in the mirror and wonder who you're supposed to be tonight. (*She takes Madam's hand*) You were always so different when he wasn't there. Everyone saw that. You could be warm and funny. Yet, as soon as he walked in, you became as shy and awkward as I was ...

Madam (*rising and taking her cup to the table*) I don't want to talk about it. It's over.

Ursula Are we similar — you and I?

Madam (*laughing*) Heaven forbid! You have many of his infuriating ways. No wonder that endless line of lovers always left you.

Ursula But I don't miss them, Mother. Especially now. And there we are alike; I wouldn't want anyone feeling sorry for me either.

Madam What will you do? Where will you go?

Ursula I shall stay at home. I love my little cottage. You've never been, have you? It's quiet, peaceful; no traffic, no people. I shall work quietly in my garden and wait until the call comes.

Madam I need someone to do my garden, as you see; it's grown as mad as I have.

Ursula It is a mess, I must admit.

Madam You could do it. Doris would make the tea. I could look after you.

Ursula Thank you, Mother ... but no. I prefer the silence of Sussex. I'd miss the sea.

We hear the front door open

Doris (*off*) Don't panic, it's only me. Would you believe I got caught in all that rain ...

Doris enters dressed for the rain and carrying an umbrella. She sees Ursula and her face registers that she does not like her

Oh, Gawd help us, look what the wind's blown in!

Ursula Hallo, Doris.

Doris Well, all I hope is you haven't been upsetting her. It's me who bears the brunt, remember.

Madam (*her old self again*) Oh, do stop moaning, woman!

Doris (*coldly*) Excuse me — I'll just get out of these wet things.

Doris exits to the kitchen

Ursula Oh, dear, perhaps I ought to be going.

Madam (*loudly*) This is my house — the woman's only a servant!

Doris (*off, calling*) I can hear you; I'm not deaf, you know.

Madam Perhaps I could come to you, Ursula.

Ursula I couldn't stand it, Mother. You'd only be a nuisance.

Madam I could make hot soup when it's cold — treacle toffee and ginger-snaps — just like the old days.

Ursula I need to be alone. I need to think things over.

Madam I'd make a log fire when the evenings start to draw in; I could be a mother to you, Ursula.

Doris enters, putting on her overall

Doris You haven't even touched your lunch.

Madam It was inedible.

Doris (*picking up the chocolate*) And what's this? Now what did the doctor say only this morning?

Ursula It's all right, Doris, it's mine. (*She takes the bar of chocolate from Doris and pockets it*)

Madam holds out her hand in a hopeless gesture, desperate to retrieve the chocolate but unable, of course, to say anything in front of Doris

Doris You should know better than to tempt her. She's a shocker when it comes to chocolate. I just thank Gawd she don't drink — otherwise we'd all have *that* to put up with!

Ursula How's Dolly?

Doris Just the same. I can see what's going to happen. I can spot it a mile off. I'll no sooner be rid of your mother than I'll have Dolly round my neck. I hope you're not expecting something to eat — I haven't catered for company.

Ursula No, no. I shall be on my way soon.

Doris Good, 'cause I've got to get your mother ready for the matinee. (*To Madam*) It's Saturday, remember. Two shows today. Excuse me.

Doris exits into the hall

Ursula Matinee? What is she on about?

Madam Now you see what I have to put up with. One can but humour her.

Ursula I'm pleased I came, Mother. I had my doubts, but it was an easier goodbye than I'd imagined. Please destroy the letter; I'd rather Doris didn't know.

Madam Shall I write? Phone? How will I know?

Ursula You'll know. When the time comes.

Madam Are you happy? I must know that.

Ursula I'm fine. At least now my time's my own. No more chasing round the country in those ghastly plays, playing to twelve people at a Wednesday matinee, lousy hotel rooms in unwelcoming towns, or lonely midnight meals of beans on toast. No more lines to learn — what absolute bliss.

Madam It's hard to face life without a little imagination, Ursula, without a tiny spotlight. I wish I were as brave as you.

Ursula You will be — and perhaps sooner than you think.

Madam I'm sorry if you think I was to blame for your unhappiness. I did only what I thought was best. Your father always wanted you to be a great actress.

Ursula He must have died disappointed.

Madam I'm not sure I care any more. Charles Penwarren — Ursula, really! I played Beatrice to his Benedick in Bristol. He was useless.

Ursula (*laughing*) You've always judged everyone by their acting ability, Mother.

Doris enters and hears the following

If it's any consolation, he was useless in bed, too.

Doris I see. That's all you ever get in this house. Dirty, smutty theatrical talk.

Madam You shouldn't be listening.

Doris (*to Ursula*) At least you sound happy. I expect, knowing her, you got what you came for.

Ursula Yes, Doris. I got what I came for. Goodbye, Mother.

Ursula and Madam embrace

You know where I am. Goodbye, Doris. Take care of her.

Ursula turns and leaves the room. The front door slams

Doris Bloomin' sauce. Did you hear that? Take care of you — a fat lot she cares.

Madam (*sitting*) I'm peckish — I need my lunch.

Doris All right, keep your hair on.

Doris exits to the kitchen as she says the following

But you'll have to hurry; you know you don't usually eat before you go on stage.

Madam picks up Ursula's letter, tears it in half and hides the pieces in her dress

(*Off*) And we don't want indigestion on top of everything else, do we?

Doris enters with a cold lunch on a tray

What are we playing today?

Doris sets out Madam's lunch on the table, clearing away the tea things that are still there

All I'm saying is you don't want to be late. You know you like
to be in the theatre by the half. (*She turns to go back to the
kitchen with the tea things*)

Madam Doris.

Doris (*stopping and turning*) Yes, Madam?

Madam Doris, I've reached a decision.

Doris Oh, yes, Madam.

Madam I'm not going on this afternoon.

Doris (*worried*) I beg your pardon.

Madam Get the understudy. She can go on in my place.

Doris The understudy. But, Madam, you've never missed a
performance in your life.

Madam I shall not be going on this evening either. I've given
up the theatre. I'm sick of it.

Doris (*ashen*) Oh, my Gawd, this is it. Shall I fetch the doctor,
Madam? Have you got a pain?

Madam (*moving to the table*) I'm perfectly well, thank you. In
fact — I've never felt better in my life!

The music creeps in

Madam sits at the table and prepares to eat her lunch

The music swells

CURTAIN

FURNITURE AND PROPERTY LIST

On stage: Two armchairs
Chaise longue
Dining table. *On it*: tablecloth, breakfast food, crockery and cutlery including a plate of scrambled eggs
Copy of *The Times*

Off stage: Tray (**Doris**)
Hoover (practical) (**Doris**)
Four letters (**Doris**)
Tea towel (**Doris**)
Doctor's bag. *In it*: stethoscope, pad, pen (**Doctor**)
Clean bed linen (**Doris**)

Personal: **Madam**: glasses (used throughout)

In Black-out p. 10

Set: **Sylvia's** coat, hat and bag. *In bag*: large bar of fruit and nut chocolate

Off stage: Wooden tray. *On it*: tea cups and milk jug (**Sylvia**)
Teapot (**Ursula**)
Umbrella (**Doris**)
Tray. *On it*: cold lunch, cutlery etc. (**Doris**)

Personal: **Ursula**: cigarette and bag

LIGHTING PLOT

Practical fittings required: nil.
Interior with exterior backdrop. The same scene throughout

To open: Darkness

EFFECTS PLOT

Cue 10   **Ursula** looks across at **Madam**   (Page 20)
          Music fades

Cue 11   **Ursula**: '... your tea's getting cold.'   (Page 24)
          Pause; then clock strikes quarter past

Cue 12   **Madam** '... better in my life!'   (Page 31)
          Music creeps in

Cue 13   **Madam** sits at the table   (Page 31)
          Music swells